MYSTERY EXPLORERS™

SEARCHING FOR

YETI

THE ABOMINABLE SNOWMAN

rosen publishing's
rosen
central

New York

Turin Truet and
Laura Anne Gilman

Published in 2012 by The Rosen Publishing Group, Inc.
29 East 21st Street, New York, NY 10010

First Edition

Library of Congress Cataloging-in-Publication Data

Truet, Turin.
Searching for Yeti: the abominable snowman/Turin Truet, Laura Anne Gilman.—1st ed.
    p. cm.—(Mystery explorers)
Includes bibliographical references and index.
ISBN 978-1-4488-4764-8 (libray binding)—
ISBN 978-1-4488-4773-0 (pbk.)—
ISBN 978-1-4488-4781-5 (6-pack)
1. Yeti—Juvenile literature. I. Gilman, Laura Anne. II. Title.
QL89.2.Y4T78 2012
001.944—dc22

2011006078

Manufactured in the United States of America

CPSIA Compliance Information: Batch #S11YA: For further information, contact Rosen Publishing, New York, New York, at 1-800-237-9932.

CONTENTS

INTRODUCTION

The Yeti, also known as the Abominable Snowman, is a creature of legend and conjecture, a giant ape-creature living in the snowy Himalayas (the mountains in south Asia). "It was a creature not much taller than a man, but broader in the shoulders, and covered with heavy white hair. It walked upright, but lurched forward in all, a most terrifying sight," according to one anonymous quote. Still, scientists and folklorists alike generally accept that myths often arise from at least a germ of fact. So, how much of what people have heard over the years about the Yeti is actually true?

The word "Yeti" has been attributed to several sources. Some claim that it comes from the Tibetan words *Yah*, meaning "rock," and *Teh*, meaning "animal"—combining to form "rock animal," perhaps for the Yeti's resemblance to a huge snow-covered boulder. Other sources say that it is from the word for "magical creature," which it must have seemed to be to the local peoples who live in the foothills of the Himalayas.

The Himalayas run along the border between India, Nepal, and Tibet, and have been referred to as the roof of the world. This is a place so distant and mysterious that it seems to be not of this Earth—exotic, dangerous, and, to many people, of great spiritual significance. Much of the remote and forbidding land around these rough peaks is uninhabited. There are some wild animals that live in the region, including tigers, leopards, deer, bears, goats, and wolves.

Sometimes strange tracks are found in the snow, possibly made by bears—or are they made by the Yeti?

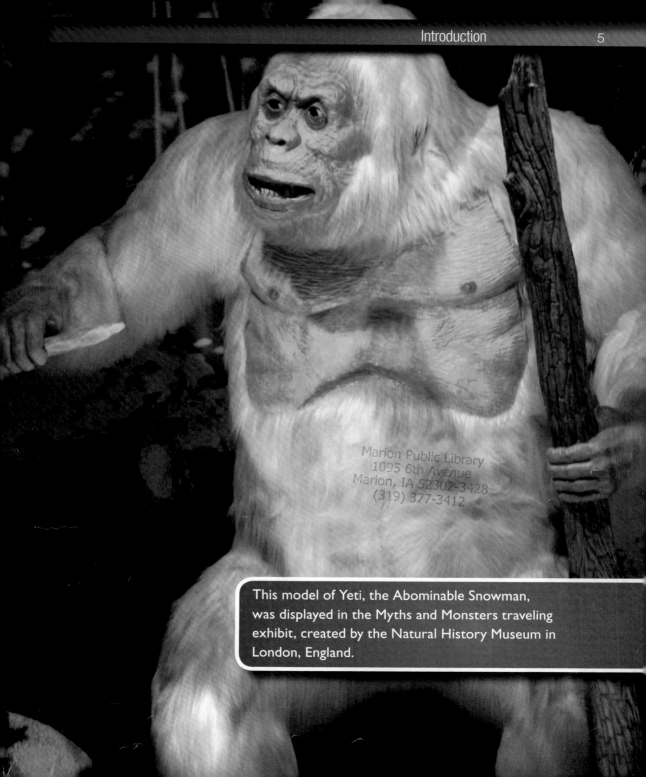

This model of Yeti, the Abominable Snowman, was displayed in the Myths and Monsters traveling exhibit, created by the Natural History Museum in London, England.

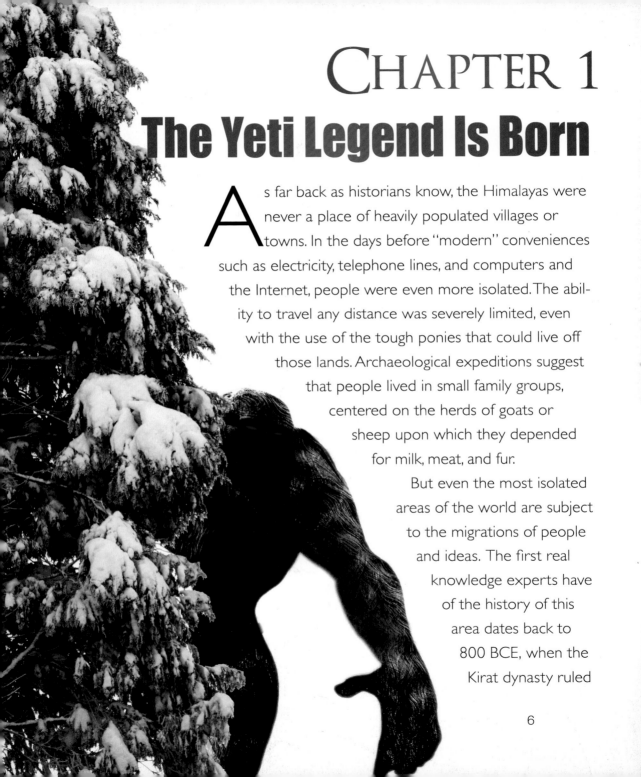

CHAPTER 1
The Yeti Legend Is Born

As far back as historians know, the Himalayas were never a place of heavily populated villages or towns. In the days before "modern" conveniences such as electricity, telephone lines, and computers and the Internet, people were even more isolated. The ability to travel any distance was severely limited, even with the use of the tough ponies that could live off those lands. Archaeological expeditions suggest that people lived in small family groups, centered on the herds of goats or sheep upon which they depended for milk, meat, and fur.

But even the most isolated areas of the world are subject to the migrations of people and ideas. The first real knowledge experts have of the history of this area dates back to 800 BCE, when the Kirat dynasty ruled

6

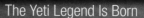

Mount Everest is the tallest mountain in the world, measuring 29,028 feet (8,848 meters) high. It is part of the Himalayas and lies half in Nepal and half in Tibet.

Tibet. It was also during this time that Buddhism—brought from India by traveling monks, traders, and scholars to the royal court—came to the foothills of the Himalayas.

After 300 CE, more people began traveling from neighboring India to Tibet. They brought with them a more sophisticated culture of record keeping and the minting of money. They also brought their religion, Hinduism. This was a time when architecture and decorative arts such as sculpture flourished in the Himalayas. In short, the society had time for leisure.

The British Step In

In the thirteenth century, British traders and explorers arrived in China and India, and Western influences began to creep in. Once in the area, the British never quite went home again, and in 1600 the British East India Company was created to simplify trade with India. One hundred and fifty years later, the British East India Company had grown to the point where it was, in effect, running the day-to-day governance of India.

But even then, with the British in charge, the Himalayas remained relatively untouched, both because they were too difficult to explore and because there was little in the region that was of financial interest to England. The locals were hired as guides and trackers, but the land itself was still a mystery.

The Sherpas

Today, the inhabitants are more connected to the rest of the world, thanks to modern means of communication. The region, however, still remains a place set apart, separated from the rest of the world by a combination of geography, politics, and climate. The local people there today are the Sherpas, who originated in Tibet, having migrated over the mountains to Nepal about five centuries ago. The Sherpas were originally farmers, herders, and traders. When the Western explorers arrived, Sherpa hunters became their guides and earned a well-deserved, worldwide reputation for their mountaineering abilities. Sherpa guides are mentioned in almost every historical account of attempts to climb Mount Everest.

These Sherpa climbers make their way toward their base camp near Mount Everest in Nepal. Throughout history, the Sherpas have been admired for their legendary strength and climbing skills during high-altitude expeditions in the Himalayas.

LIEUTENANT COLONEL CHARLES HOWARD-BURY

Born in Ireland in 1881, the British soldier, botanist, and explorer Lieutenant Colonel Charles Howard-Bury led the Mount Everest Reconnaissance Expedition in 1921. Sponsored by the Royal Geographical Society and the Alpine Club, the journey was the first official expedition to Mount Everest and it was to set the groundwork for further explorations to the summit in the following year by surveying possible routes up the peak. The nine members of the expedition were Howard-Bury, Dr. A. F. R. Wollaston, Dr. Alexander M. Heron, Harold Raeburn, George Leigh Mallory, Major E. Oliver Wheeler, Guy Bullock, Major Henry T. Morshead, and Dr. Alexander M. Kellas. Kellas studied the effects of high altitudes on the physiology of the human body and was an experienced climber who traveled often with the Sherpas. Kellas died from overexertion while en route to the mountain in 1921. Howard-Bury wrote a book about the trip, entitled *Mount Everest: The Reconnaissance, 1921,* which was published in 1922. The book was important for its detailed descriptions of the Rongbuk Glacier route to the northern approaches to Everest and numerous maps. The expedition also studied the east and west approaches to Everest. But it was the group's discovery of the route via the north ridge and their recommendation of late May and early June as being the best time for climbing that was groundbreaking. The members of the group won wide acclaim for their journey. Howard-Bury himself became a popular figure and was elected to Parliament.

It was from these people, and other local groups, that the West first encountered stories of the fabled and rarely seen *metoh-kangmi*. This is another name for the Yeti. *Metoh* translates to "man-bear" and *kangmi* to snowman. The origin of the term got a little confused in 1921, when during Charles Howard-Bury's expedition to Mount Everest, many footprints were discovered in the high altitudes. According to Howard-Bury, the Sherpa guides called them the tracks of a "metch-kangmi" or "filthy snowman." At the time, Henry Newman, a reporter of the *Statesman* in Kolkata, mistranslated the term as "abominable snowman." Newman's mistranslation was brought to light by Bill Tilman, in his book, *Mount Everest 1938*. Consequently, the name Abominable Snowman began to be used for the Yeti in 1921.

CHAPTER 2
Folklore and Myth

How long has the Yeti been known to the people of the Himalayas? It is almost impossible to tell when the first report of the man-beast was made. Certainly, long before any Western observer came to Tibet or Nepal, the Yeti was already an established part of the local culture. Whether called Yeh-ti (in Tibet), Nyalmo (on the Tibetan side of the Himalayas, Alma (in Russia), Teh-lma (in Nepal), or Kra-dhan (in Nepal), and no matter how the descriptions differed—the color of the hair or how much of the creature's body it covered—all the stories agreed: the creature walked upright, had huge feet, was the size of a man but much broader, and had hair covering most of its body. What's more, it shied away from human interaction. The occasional traveler or hunter might encounter huge footprints in the snow or lose a goat under suspicious circumstances, but actual encounters were few and far between. There were, of course, claims that a Yeti—or packs of them—had damaged villages or towns, typically looking for food.

Even so, if you asked a local, he or she would be the first to assure you that these were no mere beasts. Yetis serve a purpose, they would tell you, more than any wild animal roaming for food and shelter.

According to one Sherpa legend, the Yetis were mysterious creatures that inhabited the slopes of the Himalayas, standing between mankind and the unattainable peaks of the mountains where demon-spirits lived. As such, they were beings to be wary of but not actively feared.

Anyone who claimed to have had an encounter told of it in great detail, until the event quickly passed into legend the way an unusual or terrifying experience—such as a near miss with death—might among your friends and family today. A person's reality during moments of quick or terrifying events is altered just enough (or vastly) to be different from the truth of the event. Then, in tellings to friends and family, facts become distorted: people and objects become larger and scarier; actions become more outlandish, vivid, and deadly. After time and many more tellings, each of the people, objects, and actions in the event seem to become even more dramatic. As a result, a legend is made out of an event that was not so dramatic after all. There is no way to determine what the truth of these stories is, what had been embellished over the years, and what was outright creation. The Yeti legend is much the same.

Relics

Even physical evidence is not clear-cut. Many Buddhist lamaseries—homes to religious figures called lamas, much as monasteries would house monks—claimed to have relics, or religious objects, that came from the Yetis. Shamanistic relics of these sorts were used to remind Buddhists of their connection to the world around them, both in physical and spiritual terms. In addition, stories would grow around these objects, both true and invented, to enhance their religious significance.

This is where the tradition of folklore comes from: the stretching of what might be or might have been into genuine storytelling. It is the job of the researcher to discover what among those stories is a verified encounter and what is myth, legend, or outright falsehood. David Gordon, author of *Field Guide to the Sasquatch*, wrote, "The absence of evidence is not necessarily evidence of an absence." In other words, lack of proof is no proof at all. The burden rests on both sides—believer and skeptic—to establish their cases.

Ape-man Creatures

Although the Yeti is perhaps the best known of all such ape-man creatures, there have been related phenomena all over the world.

In the United States, Americans have the aptly named Bigfoot, or Sasquatch. The American ape-creature is to be found—at least according to the stories—in many states, from Florida up to the Canadian border, but the

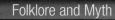

Dr. Sangay Wangchuk, director of Bhutan's conservation department, poses near the plaster casts of footprints that supposedly came from Yetis. Each footprint is about 12 inches (30.5 centimeters) in length. Like most people in Bhutan, Wangchuk, who has a master's degree from Yale University, believes in the existence of the Yeti.

best-known stomping grounds are the woods of Washington State, where its legend first grew.

But the ape man is a familiar figure in folklore—both traditional and modern—all around the world. You could start as far back as ancient Sumeria and the story of Gilgamesh, whose companion Enkidu was a "wild man" who had to be taught human speech. Or you could pick up the pages of the *National*

THE ORIGIN OF BIGFOOT

The term "Bigfoot" was first used in 1958. In the wilderness of northern California, members of a road construction company came upon some large oddly shaped tracks, which they believed were made by an apelike man. The tracks measured about 16 inches (about 41 cm) in length and about 7 inches (18 cm) in width. One of the team members, Gerald Crew, made a plaster cast of one of the prints. Reporters took photos of the plaster footprint and reproduced it in their news articles. Crew apparently came up with the name Bigfoot, and that label has been used for the North American apelike creature ever since. Ray Wallace, one of the first people to examine Crew's tracks, later admitted to using a pair of snow-shoe-sized contraptions to make the footprints over many years as a prank. In 2002, after Wallace died, his family confirmed the hoax. There were photographs showing Wallace with the devices he used in making the prints. Many other people over the years confessed to making beastlike tracks in northern California, adding to the Bigfoot folklore.

Enquirer or similar magazines and read about the latest sightings in the Pacific Northwest.

Similar sightings are everywhere. In Malaysia, 18-inch (46-cm) footprints made by a creature with a 12-foot (3.7-meter) stride were recorded in August 1966, feeding rumors of a huge ape-man living deep within the jungle. Villagers claimed the beast was a shy, harmless giant. In the Philippines, a "massive hairy creature" known as the Kapre was reported to be noxious smelling but unthreatening, and it reportedly maintained a rudimentary kind of trade agreement with local villagers. In the former Soviet Union, a creature called

A leader of the group Sasquatch Watch in Spotsylvania County, Virginia, searches for evidence of Sasquatch, or Bigfoot. There were reported sightings of the creature in the area in 2010.

Snezhni Chelovyek inspired the formation of a government research program to investigate sightings during the 1950s, but the program was later abandoned. In central Asia, close to the Yeti's home, the Alma is the local variant, which may simply be another name for the far-ranging Yeti. Moreover, in Africa, long held to be the birthplace of all humanity, there is the Waterbobbejan, or "water baboon," of South Africa, and the Agogue, a more mischievous cousin, which has been spotted in Tanzania and along the Ivory Coast.

True Story or Hoax?

In all of these cases, the descriptions of the creature remain consistent: a tall, broad-shouldered creature, more ape than man yet walking upright. The rather pungent, or powerful, body odor also remains consistent, as does an apparent lack of speech; rare is the occasion when an ape-man is heard to utter a sound, much less anything that might be considered speech. Where these stories vary is in the level of contact they have with humans, from none at all to the nighttime trading of fruits and fish in exchange for cooked goods, as reported by villagers in Malaysia. Only rarely is the ape-being considered dangerous; more often than not, the only fatalities seem to involve a sheep or goat that wandered too far from the flock and shepherd. Even the few reports of violence done to humans would appear to stem more from the creature defending its home than from any warlike or aggressive instincts.

But all of this is conjecture, based on unsubstantiated stories, rumor, and legends. Is there any scientific evidence that Yeti exists?

CHAPTER 3
Glimpses of Yeti

The official record of Yeti sightings is a slim one. If you discount secondhand reports and stories that are closer to myth than fact, it becomes even less impressive. Actually, for such a widely known creature, there isn't much to base its existence on at all. Why is that?

First of all, people need to remember that for many, many years, the Himalayas were not easily accessible to outsiders. In part, this was because of the physical isolation. The British did gain access during the nineteenth century thanks to their colonization of India. However, the trickle of British explorers never grew to a flood, and it soon ended.

But politics has been another problem. The borders

This photograph supposedly shows the footprints of the Abominable Snowman during an expedition to Mount Everest in 1961. Some experts believe that the reason there are not many images of Yeti footprints is because early camera equipment was too cumbersome to carry on mountain expeditions.

of Nepal were closed in 1816, after the country lost a war with India, and they were not opened again officially until 1951. The British occupied Tibet in 1904 and maintained control until a treaty was signed the following year. China invaded Tibet in 1950 and since then has occupied the small nation. From the beginning of the twentieth century until the end of World War II in 1945, it was almost impossible for any Westerner to enter the central Himalaya area legally. In fact, it wasn't until the 1950s that anyone was allowed back into the Himalayas, much less any scientific expeditions. Even then, the government could and did often require specific permissions that were very difficult to get. Actually, if you were to attempt to travel into Tibet today, you might find it impossible to get any sort of permission.

Yet with all these difficulties, some determined explorers did make their way into the mountains, even prior to 1950. But once they were actually on-site, why were they not able to gather more specific proof of the Yeti's existence?

First, remember the landscape. Ranging from 22,000 to 29,000 feet (6,706 to 8,839 m) above sea level, the Himalayas are inhospitable to those not accustomed to high altitudes, making travel a slow, careful business. Winters are harsh, and spring brings with it the heavy rains known as monsoons, which can create flash floods and mudslides. One bad storm could wipe out half your party if you weren't ready for it. Second, there's the technology. Prior to 1950, cameras were large, bulky, expensive machines that were difficult to work properly in extreme temperatures, assuming the delicate pieces made it safely up the mountainside. Unlike today's point-and-shoot digital cameras and cell phone cameras, those earlier models needed training to

SOME RECORDED SIGHTINGS OF YETI AROUND THE WORLD

1832 B. H. Hodson, a British representative to Nepal, reports an attack on his native guides by creatures that the locals referred to as "rakshas," or demons. These creatures were described as being more catlike that apelike.

1889 Major L. A. Waddell, while exploring the area of northeast Sikkim in the Himalayas, reports finding large bearlike footprints in the snow well above the elevation at which any bear should be living. His Sherpa guides tell him it is a Yeti, a hairy and dangerous beast that feeds on humans.

1913 A strange, very strong creature with a black monkey-like face and body covered in long silvery yellow fur is reportedly captured by Chinese hunters. The creature had hands and feet like a man. It dies after five months in captivity.

1921 Members of an expedition led by Lieutenant Colonel Charles Howard-Bury spot figures ahead of them while climbing Mount Everest. They find huge footprints of someone—or something—walking barefoot in the snowfield.

1923 Major Alan Cameron, of an Everest expedition, reports seeing a line of figures moving along a cliff above the snowline. Two days later, photos are taken of footprints.

1925 N. A. Tombazi, while exploring Sikkim in the Himalayas, glimpses a creature ahead of him, some 15,000 feet (4,572 m) up the side of Mount Everest. He said the humanlike creature, which was not wearing clothing, walked upright and was dark against the snow.

1936 Footprints are found in the outer reaches of the snowline by members of the H. W. Tilman expedition while nearing Mount Everest.

1937 Explorer Frank Smythe, on a return trip from Tibet, reports finding tracks at the 14,000-foot (4,267-m) level, which local Tibetans and Sherpas said were left by the hairy wild men.

1948 A Norwegian prospector, Jan Frostis, claims to have been attacked by one of two Yetis, in one of the rare physical encounters, while near Zemu Gap, in Sikkim. His shoulder is badly mangled.

1950 Mummified fingers and some skin are found in

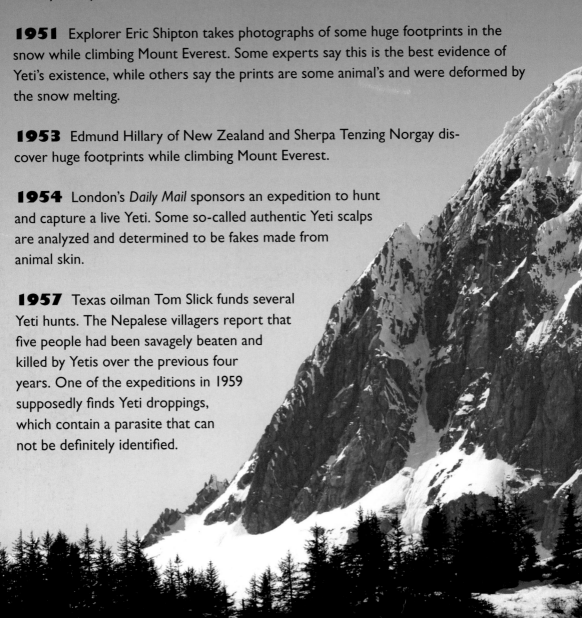

the Himalayas. Experts determine that the body parts are "almost human" but cannot identify the species.

1951 Explorer Eric Shipton takes photographs of some huge footprints in the snow while climbing Mount Everest. Some experts say this is the best evidence of Yeti's existence, while others say the prints are some animal's and were deformed by the snow melting.

1953 Edmund Hillary of New Zealand and Sherpa Tenzing Norgay discover huge footprints while climbing Mount Everest.

1954 London's *Daily Mail* sponsors an expedition to hunt and capture a live Yeti. Some so-called authentic Yeti scalps are analyzed and determined to be fakes made from animal skin.

1957 Texas oilman Tom Slick funds several Yeti hunts. The Nepalese villagers report that five people had been savagely beaten and killed by Yetis over the previous four years. One of the expeditions in 1959 supposedly finds Yeti droppings, which contain a parasite that can not be definitely identified.

handle and proper conditions in order to get the best results. At the upper levels of Mount Everest, the air temperature can get dangerously cold, down to -4°Fahrenheit (-20°Celsius). In addition, the higher up you go, the colder and more bitterly dry the air becomes. It's not healthy for people, and most certainly it was no good for photographic film. For that reason, most of the

In 1980, Igor Burtsev, director of the International Center of Hominology, compares his foot size with that of a cast made of a footprint discovered in the Pamirs, a mountain range in central Asia. Burtsev has headed several expeditions to search for Yetis, including in Siberia.

historical evidence comes from written journals and sketches, with only the occasional black-and-white photograph of a footprint.

Modern expeditions, it might be assumed, would take with them modern equipment, allowing a much more accurate means to capture what proof they might find. This, however, is not often the case. Although the technology has advanced, the cost for such tools has increased. Even though the explorers of the previous century, and the scientists of the first half of the twentieth century, often had government backing to fund their supplies, modern Yeti researchers all too often are working on a nonprofit basis, either on their own or through an organization that does not have the funds to outfit them properly. The exceptions, such as the Slick and the *Daily Mail* expeditions, will be discussed in the next chapter.

CHAPTER 4
Examining the Evidence

R eading the accounts of past explorers searching for the Yeti, it may seem as though they went in without planning or preparation. Their expeditions seemed doomed to failure. But in the late 1950s, a series of organized explorations were launched after the Nepalese and Tibetan governments opened their borders to outsiders once again.

Shipton's Yeti Footprint Photos

Eric Shipton was an experienced explorer, with half a dozen attempts to climb Mount Everest

This picture of a footprint, reportedly from a Yeti, was taken in 1951 by Eric Shipton while in the Menlung basin in the Himalayas. Many experts believe this image is the best evidence that an Abominable Snowman exists.

under his belt. In the winter of 1951, he and two companions were working their way across a neighboring mountain. They spotted a figure moving in the distance ahead of them, 20,000 feet (nearly 6 kilometers) up on the slopes of the Menlung Glacier. They tracked the Yeti until it disappeared into an ice field. Shipton took a photograph of the creature's footprints. Those photos clearly showed the imprint of a foot that could have been that of a Yeti, an unknown animal, or a bear.

Photographed with an ice ax next to it, the clearest footprint measured 12 inches (30.5 cm) long by 6 inches (15.2 cm) wide. These footprints were not made by a human. The Shipton photograph is often held up as one of the best pieces of evidence of something living in the heights of the Himalayas.

Other Unusual Investigations

Between 1951 and 1953, René de Nebesky-Wojkowitz, an Austrian ethnologist and Tibetologist, fielded several Yeti explorations to Tibet. He also wrote a book entitled *Oracles and Demons of Tibet*, which was published in 1956. The members of the excursions found nothing but some tracks that didn't look like any known animal living in the area. Nebesky-Wojkowitz suggested that this failure was due to the Yeti's superior mobility over rough terrain and an increased lung capacity that gave it an impressive advantage in those high, oxygen-starved elevations.

The *Daily Mail*, a British newspaper, funded a survey in 1954. Zoologists, naturalists, cameramen, and trained guides formed the expedition. They found

GORILLAS OR HOLY MEN?

Some skeptics of the Yeti insist that the so-called Yeti footprints that have been discovered in the snow of the Himalayas over the years are actually animal tracks that were misshapened as the snow melted. As prints melt, they become larger. Other doubters believe that the prints are those of holy men who at times go barefoot. The supposed Yeti scalps that are collected in monasteries in Nepal and Tibet are likely made of goatskin. Some monks recount that the scalps are ancient religious objects that were made as wigs and were worn by dancers who played Yeti characters in rituals.

tracks and droppings, which they claimed came from a Yeti, plus a scalp of coarse hair that was unlike human hair. The expedition was allowed to take one hair from that scalp out of the country, but no more. Test results on its origin were inconclusive.

In 1954, American scientist Dr. Norman Dyrenfurth discovered caves in Kathmandu, Nepal, that showed evidence of having been inhabited by near-human creatures. He had plaster casts of footprints and hair samples as evidence. The results of testing on these samples at that time were still open to question.

The Slick Excursions

In 1956, Thomas Slick, a Texas oilman and millionaire with a longtime interest in trying to discover the truth behind the Yeti legend, gained the backing of the San Antonio Zoo. Such sponsorship allowed Slick's party to enter the Himalayas in 1957 as a legitimate, government-approved expedition. Thanks to Slick's money, the expedition came equipped with up-to-date scientific equipment, weapons, hounds to track the Yeti's scent, and enough men to cover a large area and question locals. Those interviews led Slick to speculate that there were actually two or three different types of Yetis, each living in a different area of Tibet.

He and his crews made several trips into the mountains between 1957 and 1959, coming back with photos, footprint castings, and—in a rather brazen act of smuggling that involved the aid of American actor James Stewart and his wife—two fingers from a mummified hand that locals claimed was that of a Yeti. Called the Pangboche hand for the location it was taken from, Slick's team replaced the stolen fingers with human ones so their theft would not be quickly noticed, then slipped the mummified digits into the luggage of the Stewarts, trusting that the luggage of such world-famous people would not be searched.

The Stewarts arrived safely in London, but their luggage didn't! It was lost between flights, and the scientists had to assume that even if the luggage was found, their prized piece of evidence would be discovered and confiscated. However, the luggage was returned to the Stewarts soon after, still unsearched.

So what happened to all this evidence? No one is quite sure. Loren Coleman, in his book *Tom Slick and the Search for the Yeti*, mentions that a footprint cast and hair were reportedly sent to *Life* magazine, which had been "consulting" with Slick on his discoveries. It may be that they are still stored somewhere in a warehouse, unmarked and forgotten.

A preserved skull and skeleton hand are seen here on display at the Pangboche monastery, near Mount Everest. Many people believed that the artifacts were from a Yeti. Sir Edmund Hillary determined in 1961 that the artifacts were a hoax.

Efforts to Disprove the Yeti Myth

The Slick expeditions should have been enough to make the search for the Yeti a respected scientific venture. But Sir Edmund Hillary, renowned as the first Westerner to climb Mount Everest, was determined to debunk the Yeti myth once and for all.

In 1960, a scientific expedition sponsored by World Book, Inc., went into the Himalayas, led by Sir Edmund Hillary and Marlin Perkins, who would in later years star in the nature documentary TV series *Wild Kingdom*. During their three months in the field, they investigated the "proof" Slick's team claimed to have found. Furthermore, it was here that the Pangboche hand came back to haunt Tom Slick. With the human fingers added, its veracity—along with that of other pelts and scalps—was thrown into serious doubt. In addition, Hillary publicly disputed the words of his former guide, the Sherpa Sen Tensing, saying, "He . . . had been attending the three-day Mani Rimdu ceremony . . . one that I knew by experience ended in a carnival atmosphere with much drinking of beer and spirits."

In other words, Sen Tensing was an unreliable witness because he was in a location where alcohol was being consumed. There was no evidence that Sen Tensing himself had been drinking or was in any way incapacitated, but the implication, from such a respected figure, was enough. The World Book expedition's report that the Yeti was nothing more than a myth was more newsworthy than Slick's claims to the contrary, and they had the weight of public opinion on their side, including articles in *Life* and *National Geographic*, among others, and a traveling road show in the mid-1960s featuring Perkins and Hillary.

An Accidental Sighting

In 1970, a British expedition led by Chris Bonington attempted to climb the south face of Annapurna (the tenth-highest mountain in the world, also located in the Himalayas). Bonington chose Dougal Haston and Don Whillans to be a part of the expedition. Haston and Whillans reached the summit on May 27, 1970. Although the trip was unrelated to hunting the Yeti, members of the team found a series of footprints in areas known to have no human habitation and no known population of large animals such as bears. Whillans reported observing through his binoculars a black humanoid creature in the moonlight for about twenty minutes before losing sight of it.

But by the 1970s, the wave of public opinion had turned. The hunt for the Yeti had been recast from scientific exploration to the foolishness of crackpots.

CHAPTER 5
Science Comes to the Rescue

The evidence presented in defense of the existence of the Yeti has been, at best, sketchy. Reported sightings, blurred photographs, casts of footprints that may or may not have been created by known animals such as bears, or the possibility of an outright hoax have not helped to prove the Yeti's existence. The few unidentified pieces of physical evidence are just dubious enough for them to be justifiably dismissed from consideration by the rational eye of a skeptic.

The urge, in fact, is often to dismiss Yeti sightings the same way many scientists dismiss UFO sightings or the existence of the Loch Ness monster. The

35

Cryptozoology

Cryptozoology is the study of and search for animals, especially those that are from legends and myths, such as Yeti and Bigfoot, to evaluate the likelihood of their existence. The word "cryptozoology" originated with Dr. Bernard Heuvelmans (1916–2001), a zoologist, jazz musician, comedian, and writer. The word apparently comes from the Greek word *kryptos*, which means "hidden" or "mysterious," and *zoology*, the study of animals. The word then refers to the study of hidden animals. Heuvelmans researched and studied various animals, trying to scientifically substantiate or debunk various rumors and legends over the years. In 1999, he donated his extensive documentation and specimens to the Museum of Zoology in Lausanne, Switzerland.

pursuit of truth would be much easier if experts could just write off every person who saw a distorted footprint in the snow or caught a glimpse of what might have been an upright, manlike figure lumbering off into the distance. But the mark of a true scientist is one who doesn't discard any theory or claim, no matter how crazy it may sound, until it has been proved untrue. Many of the scientific findings experts now take as self-evident—fossils, for example—were once held to be hoaxes or mistaken identifications. Lack of proof cannot be taken as proof of nonexistence. It is for those reasons that science has not yet been able to close the books on the Yeti.

Yes, all the sightings might just be the result of hallucinations caused by the high altitude and resulting lack of oxygen or charlatans looking to pull a scam and make money off of their celebrity. But what of those footprints, the unidentifiable droppings and hairs, the photographs and videotapes of footprints, the long history of consistent reporting by many people? Is it possible that the Yeti, rather than simply being a figment of people's imaginations, is actually an identifiable, natural part of the world?

The Assumptions

Some researchers claim that the Yeti and its kin around the world are "wild men," perhaps direct descendants of the first primates to come out of Africa, and evolved into having intelligence that was near to that of humans. Others think that the Yeti is a modern but not yet identified ape, a closer relative to the gorilla than to humans. But one of the most plausible scenarios offered to date involves *Gigantopithecus. Gigantopithecus* was the largest primate to live

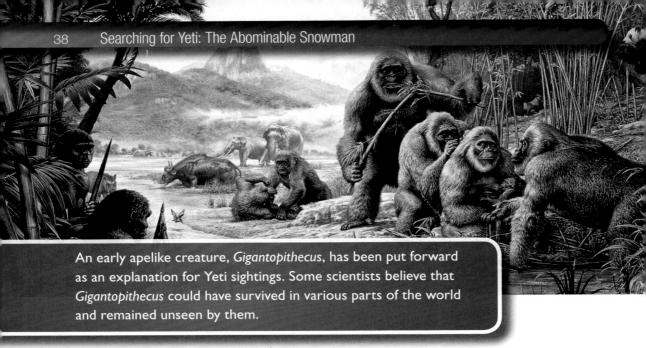

An early apelike creature, *Gigantopithecus*, has been put forward as an explanation for Yeti sightings. Some scientists believe that *Gigantopithecus* could have survived in various parts of the world and remained unseen by them.

on Earth. It stood almost 10 feet (3 m) high and weighed close to 600 pounds (272 kilograms). This great ape lived during the Pleistocene era, 1.8 million to 10,000 years ago. The fossil record from that time shows that it lived in the area that is now China and Southeast Asia.

According to scientists, *Gigantopithecus* looked very much like today's gorilla, not walking upright on two feet, but using arms and knuckles to cover ground more efficiently on four limbs. Fossil records also suggest that its dietary habits were much the same as its modern descendants—mostly vegetarian. If so, scientists can assume that its behavior might also mimic that of modern gorillas: shy and retiring creatures that nonetheless can become quite aggressive when they are threatened. Some animals that have survived from the time of the *Gigantopithecus* include the orangutan and tapir of southeastern Asia and the giant panda.

There are enough similarities in appearance and overlap in territory that the link between the Yeti and *Gigantopithecus* cannot be dismissed out of hand. Is it possible that a branch of this ancient family did not die out some five hundred thousand years ago, as always thought?

Because there is no obvious reason why *Gigantopithecus* became extinct, save for a probable failure to adapt to changes in the climate during the Ice Age, it is possible that such a branch does exist. Certainly the remoteness of the region would aid such a race in remaining undiscovered until only recently. This would explain the scant reports of such creatures until the nineteenth century.

The arguments against this theory are that *Gigantopithecus* theoretically stood between 8 (2.4 m) and 10 feet (3 m) tall, while the Yeti reportedly average 5 feet (1.5 m) tall—barely the size of an adult human. It is possible that the species might have shrunk, but such a great difference between those average heights makes this seem unlikely.

Other researchers claim that the Yeti might be a descendant of humans' own ancestor, the Neanderthal. The height would certainly be a better match, but the reported hairiness of the Yeti gives pause: Neanderthals would have been no hairier than an average *Homo sapiens*, or modern humans. Both these theories take a heavy blow when faced with the fact that the last Neanderthal has been dated at 40,000 BCE, and *Gigantopithecus* was last seen in the fossil record at five hundred thousand years ago. Without more recent fossil records, it is almost impossible to draw a connection that will stand up to scientific scrutiny.

The skulls displayed at an evolution exhibit are hominid fossils, primates of the family Hominidae, which includes modern humans and their extinct precursors. Some people think that the Yeti might be descended from a branch of the humans' family tree from three million years ago.

A New Genus?

In 1999, a group of paleontologists led by Dr. Maeve Leakey found a skull and partial jawbone in northern Kenya, in Africa. After careful study, it was determined that the nearly complete skull was 3.5 million years old and belonged to a completely different genus and species than they had expected. Dr. Leakey named the new genus *Kenyanthropus platyops* (meaning, "flat-faced man of Kenya"). However, some scientists classify the fossil as a separate species of *Australopithecus*. Whereas before, scientists thought that modern *Homo sapiens* had descended from Lucy (*Australopithecus afarensis*), the fossil species that dated back 3.5 to 4 million years, it now may be that humans' family tree has a great many branches—and the founding parent of humans' own specific branch is in doubt. If this is the case, then who is to say that the Yeti cannot exist— and in fact, may be a cousin of humans, descended from a three-million-year-old branch?

According to Dr. Leakey, when hominids split off from the great apes and began walking upright, it would make sense that they would wander into different territories and adapt to their new homes. If one of these offshoot branches were to have wandered from Africa into the highlands of Asia, it would certainly have developed a coat of hair to protect itself from the cold; larger feet, like a snowshoe rabbit, to run along the surface of the snow; and many other characteristics that could describe the Yeti.

In short, just when people think science has given them an answer, new discoveries cast light on old evidence and make people question their previous conclusions.

CHAPTER 6
Contemporary Yeti Studies

I n 2004, Henry Gee, the senior editor of *Nature*, an international weekly science journal, wrote an article entitled "Flores, God and Cryptozoology." In the article he implied that the discovery of some fossils called *Homo floresiensis* ("Flores Man" and nicknamed the Hobbit) on the island of Flores in Indonesia in 2004 could raise the hopes of Yeti hunters. *Homo floresiensis*, a potential dwarf-size relative of humans, is now extinct. The small human relative lived about eighteen thousand years ago. According to Gee, "The discovery that *Homo floresiensis* survived until so very recently, in geological terms, makes it more likely that stories of other mythical, humanlike creatures such as yetis are founded on grains of truth."

Unshakeable Inquisitors

Joshua Gates and his team, who work on a television series called *Destination Truth*, reported discovering footprints in Nepal, in the area near Mount Everest in December 2007. (Episodes of *Destination Truth*, which is shown on the cable channel Syfy, formerly known as the Sci-Fi Channel, take viewers around the world to investigate paranormal phenomena and unexplained creatures.) The team made plaster casts of the footprints, and a scientist at Idaho State University studied them. Gates said that the scientist did not believe that the prints were made by humans or by a bear. He did think, though, that they were humanlike. In 2009, Gates's team found hair from a creature in Bhutan. A forensics laboratory in Texas examined the hair samples and concluded that they were from a primate, one that has not yet been identified by scientists.

British scientists found hairs in the Garo Hills area of northeast India in July 2008 and had them analyzed by the Oxford Brookes University in England. Originally, the tests were inconclusive. The samples were found to be similar to those collected by Hillary's expedition group in the 1950s. Lab analyses have since revealed that the hair came from the Himalayan goral, also called a gray goral. This mammal looks like a brownish gray or reddish goat and has backward-curving, pointed horns.

In October 2008, members of a Japanese expedition to the Himalayan region of Nepal and Tibet photographed footprints that they believe might have

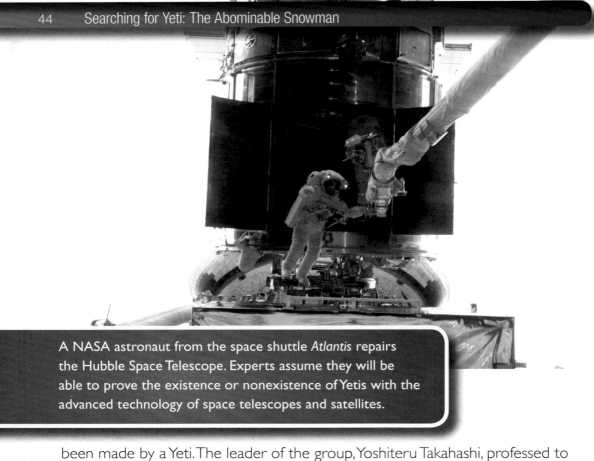

A NASA astronaut from the space shuttle *Atlantis* repairs the Hubble Space Telescope. Experts assume they will be able to prove the existence or nonexistence of Yetis with the advanced technology of space telescopes and satellites.

been made by a Yeti. The leader of the group, Yoshiteru Takahashi, professed to have seen a Yeti on a journey he made five years earlier. He described the creature as being half-man and half-ape. He said the creature walked on two legs like a human and stood about 5 feet (150 cm) tall. Takahashi said that the team would continue to hunt for the Yeti until they capture the creature on film.

So Where Is the Proof?

What all the reports prove at the moment is that there is no proof, one way or the other, to decide the Yeti question once and for all. If you choose to

YETI PROJECT JAPAN

According to the *Guardian* newspaper in the United Kingdom in October 2008, a team of Japanese adventurers, called Yeti Project Japan, believe that they found footprints of the mythological Abominable Snowman. The prints measured about 8 inches (20 cm) long and were humanlike in appearance. The Japanese explorers discovered the prints at an altitude of about 15,748 feet (4,800 m) on Dhaulagiri IV, a mountain in the subrange of the Himalayas in western Nepal. According to a team member, "We saw three footprints which looked like that of human beings." The team spent more than forty days on Dhaulagiri IV, which is about 25,135 feet (7,661 m) high. The explorers said that they had seen a Yeti in the past, although they could not provide a single photograph as proof. They did take photos of the footprints, though. The team intends to keep searching for the Yeti, and they are convinced that sooner or later someone will be able to prove its existence.

believe in the Yeti, the evidence seems beyond doubt. If you choose to be skeptical, the stories are flimsy, and the evidence is unreliable.

However, there is still the possibility that, in the not too distant future, science will be able to conclusively prove the existence—or nonexistence—of the Yeti. With the fine-tuning of such technology as spectrographics (the ability to find objects or individuals through the heat they generate naturally) and satellites, scientists may soon be able to determine if any man-sized creatures live in the heights of the Himalayas.

But it's not enough to simply discover if something lives there. A heat signature of that size might be a bear or a reclusive human.

Scientists need to identify what it is that lives out there. All they need to do is retrieve new, uncontaminated samples of alleged Yeti skin or hair.

But perhaps rather than *when*, it should be *if* experts retrieve new samples. The Yeti has proved elusive for many years, and in recent years the Chinese government took down an offered bounty payable on evidence of the Yeti, perhaps fearing a repeat of what happened with the giant panda, or worse, the total destruction of the creature's habitat, which might lead to its inevitable extinction. Unlike the explorers of the nineteenth and early twentieth centuries, people understand the delicate balance of nature, even if they don't always work within it. It may be that, like the giant panda, the Yeti is slow to breed and slow to recover from human incursions. It is possible that, like so many other animals discovered post-extinction, they have already died out, and the scraps people have are all that remains.

Joshua Gates *(right)* of the TV show *Destination Truth* and a Nepali guide are shown here in 2007 holding a cast of a footprint supposedly made by a Yeti in the region of Mount Everest. After testing some hair samples collected in the area, scientists found that they were from an unidentified primate.

Outwitting Humans

If not, it may be that the Yeti has outsmarted humans in their fumblings to find physical evidence of its existence. After avoiding contact with humans for hundreds of years, thriving in an otherwise inhospitable location, perhaps the Yeti has also perfected the art of concealment, remaining one step ahead of those who would capture it. The Yeti has remained a myth for thousands of years, after all, despite humans' most determined efforts. Perhaps it will always remain so.

CHAPTER 7

Yeti in Pop Culture, Music, Film, and Literature

The Yeti or Abominable Snowman has been featured in numerous ways throughout the decades. It has become a popular icon in advertisements, amusement and theme parks, music, movies, and books.

The Yeti has been used as a mascot for the Czech automobile manufacturer Skoda, which made the mini SUV Yeti beginning in 2009. Walt Disney World's Expedition Everest, an attraction at Disney's Animal Kingdom theme park in Florida has a high, fast roller coaster that includes the

48

An audio-animatronic Abominable Snowman screeches as riders whiz by on the Disneyland Matterhorn Bobsleds ride. The Abominable Snowman and Yeti creatures have been frequent characters in popular culture.

snarling creature Yeti at the mountain's summit. In addition to the roller coaster in this theme park, there is a Yak & Yeti Restaurant. In Disneyland, in California, there is a high-speed amusement ride called the Matterhorn Bobsleds that plunges riders into caves and hurls them into the air, near the dens of the audio-animatronic Abominable Snowmen who lurk and growl among the mountain's cliffs.

Music

Every year in the town of George, Washington, the Sasquatch! Music Festival is held in the Gorge Amphitheatre. The House of Blues, which operates the festival, puts on a variety of music, including indie rock, alternative rock, hip-hop, and some comedy performances. There are four stages at the festival: Sasquatch! Main Stage, Bigfoot Stage, Rumpus Room, and Yeti Stage. The festival strives to present music for every taste and is usually held at the end of May.

Various music groups have used "Yeti" in their band name, songs, or album titles, including the German rock band Amon Düül II with their second album *Yeti* (1970); the American hard rock band Clutch with their 1998 album *The Elephant Riders*, which includes the song "Yeti"; and the American heavy metal band High on Fire with their album *Surrounded by Thieves* (2002), which includes the song "The Yeti." The British rock band Yeti, which was formed in 2004, is centered in North London. Critics have compared the band's music style to the early Beatles' sound; Yeti recorded their debut album, *The Legend of Yeti Gonzales,* in 2008.

MYTHS AND MONSTERS EXHIBIT

In 2010, the Horniman Museum in London, England, put on a temporary exhibition about mythical monsters, entitled Myths and Monsters. The museum was one of several locations for the traveling exhibition, originally organized by the Natural History Museum in London. (The scientists at the Natural History Museum were the experts who analyzed the "Yeti scalp," which Sir Edmund Hillary had borrowed for further study during his expeditions to the Himalayas in the 1960s.) The display included animatronic models of the Cyclops, unicorn, Yeti, mermaid, dragon, and chimera, among other creatures. The museum took visitors on a journey to discover what was truth and what was fiction regarding the ancient myths and legends, and it presented a variety of scientific evidence that offered explanations about the myths' origins and merits. The exhibit investigated the links between dinosaurs and dragons and whether or not the Yeti could be an actual living creature.

Concertgoers at the Sasquatch! Music Festival gather around the Yeti stage in George, Washington. Music groups have used "Yeti" in band names, song titles, and lyrics.

Film

Over the years there have been several important films in which Yetis play a part. *The Snow Creature* (1954), directed by W. Lee Wilder, is about an American botanical expedition to the Himalayas where the members, including a news photographer and a local Sherpa guide whose wife is kidnapped by a Yeti, discover a Yeti den while they are searching for the guide's wife. They capture one of the creatures and take it back to Los Angeles, California, where it escapes during an argument with customs about whether the creature is an animal or a human. Meanwhile, the Yeti kills whoever gets in its way.

Director Val Guest made *The Abominable Snowman* in 1957. The plot of this movie involved an English botanist and an American scientist who journey to the Himalayas to find the legendary creature Yeti. Conflicts between the scientists come to a head after a Yeti is shot, and then the plot gets more complicated when other Yetis try to retrieve their companion.

Warner Brothers Cartoons produced some Looney Tunes episodes with Abominable Snowman or Yeti figures, particularly 1961's "The Abominable Snow Rabbit," starring Bugs Bunny and Daffy Duck. The two cartoon characters plan to dig their way underground to sunny Palm Springs, California, but take a wrong turn and end up in the snow-covered Himalayas. They run into the Abominable Snowman, who gives them some trouble and follows them to Palm Springs, where he finally melts away.

In 1964, the stop-motion animation Christmas special *Rudolph the Red-Nosed Reindeer*, aired on the NBC television network. Rudolph and his friend Hermey the Elf encounter the Abominable Snow Monster of the North while in the woods. The monster dislikes Christmas but loves to eat reindeer, and so he chases them. Eventually, the Abominable Snow Monster captures Rudolph and his family in his cave. Friends come to the rescue by clobbering the monster. Near the end of the movie, the Abominable Snow Monster has second thoughts and puts a star on the top of the Christmas tree and is welcomed in Christmastown.

Snowbeast, a made-for-television thriller that was broadcast in 1977 and directed by Herb Wallerstein, is about a ski resort in Colorado that

The Abominable Snowman was a character in Pixar and Disney's *Monsters, Inc*. The Yeti and Abominable Snowman have appeared in films, TV programs, and animated movies since the early 1950s.

is terrorized by a Bigfoot-like creature that brutally murders people on the ski slopes.

The animated *Monsters, Inc.*, produced by Pixar Animation Studios and released by Walt Disney Pictures in 2001, is about monsters who are professional scarers. The monsters sneak into children's bedrooms to make them scream. They then convert the kids' screams into energy to power Monstropolis, a city without humans, and to keep the town running. One of the monsters is the Abominable Snowman, the voice of which is supplied by actor John Ratzenberger. A little human girl accidentally enters the city, and the good, kind-hearted monsters attempt to return her to her home before the bad, mean-spirited monsters try to thwart their efforts. In the end, the monsters realize that laughter gives them more energy than do the children's screams.

Literature and Comics

R. L. Stine wrote a children's book entitled *The Abominable Snowman of Pasadena* in his Goosebumps series, which was published by Scholastic in 2003. The characters, Jordan Blake and his sister, Nicole, are tired of the heat in Pasadena, California, and end up taking a trip to Alaska, where they experience a real winter. Their father has been hired to photograph a mysterious huge snow creature known as the Abominable Snowman. The monster ends up chasing Jordan and Nicole.

In *The Adventures of Tintin*, a comic strip series, the Belgian artist George Rémi (1907–1983), who worked under the pen name Hergé, created a Yeti story, "Tintin in Tibet." The hero, a young reporter named Tintin, travels to Tibet to rescue a Chinese friend, Chang Chong-Chen, who is involved in a plane crash in the Himalayas. While in Tibet, the rescue team discovers footprints in the snow that resemble Yeti prints. After a series of mishaps, including being buried in an avalanche, the group finds Chang in a cave with the Yeti, who has befriended him. The team rescues Chang, who is convinced that the Yeti is not a wild beast, but a being with a human soul.

In the Marvel Comics Universe, the Abominable Snowman is a character, originally appearing in *Tales to Astonish*, No. 13. The story revolves around Carl Hanson who is in Calcutta, India, and overhears someone speaking about a photograph that he owns showing the Abominable Snowman. Hanson steals the photo and journeys to the Himalayas to find the monster. He doesn't get any help from the local people because they know that the photo is cursed and they recommend that Hanson get rid of it before it destroys him. Consequently, Hanson hunts for the monster himself, only to grow to resemble the Abominable Snowman as he climbs higher up into the mountains. Eventually, he loses his mind and drops the photo, which now mirrors what he has become.

In DC Comics, the fictional character Snowman, a villain, appears in *Batman*, No. 337. Snowman has a special gene that allows him to create and control snow and ice. He also has superhuman strength. Snowman, or Klaus Kristin, is the son of a male Yeti and a woman named Katrina Kristin. Snowman went to Gotham City to freeze it and runs up against Batman. In No. 522, Batman goes to Tibet to hunt the Snowman and ends up fighting him and Snowman's father, the Yeti. Snowman supposedly dies during the battle with Batman.

There are many mysterious creatures throughout history and science that defy common sense. They have fascinated people for centuries and may continue to elude those people who wish to definitely prove or disprove their existence. For skeptics, the Yeti or Abominable Snowman has never existed, and what evidence has appeared has been the result of human hoaxes. For believers, footprint tracks in the snow, photographs, and new sightings are enough to prove that ape-men creatures truly exist.

Some skeptics of the Yeti insist that the so-called Yeti footprints that have been discovered in the snow of the Himalayas over the years are actually animal tracks that were misshapened as the snow melted. As prints melt, they become larger. Other doubters believe that the prints are those of holy men who at times go barefoot. The supposed Yeti scalps that are collected in monasteries in Nepal and Tibet are likely made of goatskin. Some monks recount that the scalps are ancient religious objects that were made as wigs and were worn by dancers who played Yeti characters in rituals.

GLOSSARY

Abominable Snowman Also known as Yeti, a legendary hairy, humanoid creature that is said to live in the Himalayas.

animatronic Describes lifelike robots or models that move electronically.

Bigfoot The North American version of the Yeti, frequently spotted along the U.S. and Canadian border, especially in Washington State.

botanical Of or relating to plants.

Buddhism An Asian religion and philosophy founded in northeastern India around 525 BCE by Siddhartha Gautama, who was called the Buddha.

carnivore Animal that feeds on flesh.

conjecture An opinion or conclusion formed on the basis of incomplete information.

debunk To expose the falseness of a myth, idea, or belief.

ethnologist A scientist who studies the characteristics of various peoples and the differences and relationships between them.

genus A grouping of organisms having common characteristics distinct from those of other groupings.

Gigantopithecus An extinct genus of ape, dating back more than 500,000 years; the largest primate yet discovered.

glacier A mass of ice typically found in extremely cold climates, formed by snow that is compressed into granular ice. Glaciers move at a slow pace, pushed forward by gravity and their own weight.

Himalayas One of the greatest mountain ranges in the entire world, reaching from Pakistan through India, to Tibet and Nepal.

Hinduism A major religious and cultural tradition of India, which was developed from the Vedic religion.

hominids Humans and their primate ancestors.

Homo sapiens The species, or categorization, to which modern humans belong.

Neanderthal An ancient subspecies of *Homo sapiens*.

paranormal Relating to events or phenomena that are beyond the scope of normal scientific understanding.

Pleistocene era A time period in Earth's history, which began roughly 1.8 million years ago and ended 11,000 years ago, during which much of the world was covered by water or ice.

primate A mammal in an order that includes apes, monkeys, lemurs, and humans.

Sherpa A people living in Nepal who have a reputation for being the best mountain climbers and guides in the world.

skeptic A person who questions or doubts all accepted opinions.

Tibetologist A person who studies subjects relating to Tibet, including its history, religion, language, and culture.

Yeti The common name given to the two-legged and hairy creature frequently spotted in the Himalayas in Tibet and Nepal; also known as the Abominable Snowman.

FOR MORE INFORMATION

Bigfoot Field Researchers Organization
(408) 634-2376
Web site: http://www.bfro.net
Founded in 1995, the scientific research group explores the mystery of
    Sasquatch and Bigfoot.

Cryptomundo
Web site: http://www.cryptomundo.com
This Web site, which is maintained by leaders in the field of cryptozoology,
    shares information about Bigfoot, Yeti, the Loch Ness monster, and other
    cryptids (elusive and rare animals).

Natural History Museum
Cromwell Road
London SW7 5BD
United Kingdom
Web site: http://nhm.ac.uk
The Natural History Museum sponsored a traveling exhibition on Myths and
    Monsters and includes specimens and displays about the popular Yeti and
    Abominable Snowman.

Sasquatch Information Society
P.O. Box 48333
Seattle, WA 98148

Web site: http://www.bigfootinfo.org

This organization provides a database containing Bigfoot news, articles, links, polls, events, sightings, interviews, and research.

Texas Bigfoot Research Conservancy (TBRC)

P.O. Box 866621

Plano, TX 75086-6621

(877) 529-5550

Web site: http://www.texasbigfoot.org

The TBRC is a nonprofit scientific-research organization that pursues education and research activities involving the centuries-old "wildman" or "hairy man" phenomenon in North America.

Web Sites

Due to the changing nature of Internet links, Rosen Publishing has developed an online list of Web sites related to the subject of this book. This site is updated regularly. Please use this link to access the list:

http://www.rosenlinks.com/me/yeti

FOR FURTHER READING

Childress, David. *Yetis, Sasquatch & Hairy Giants.* Kempton, IL: Adventures Unlimited Press, 2010.

Coleman, Loren. *Bigfoot! The True Story of Apes in America.* New York, NY: Pocket Books, 2003.

Coleman, Loren. *Tom Slick: True Life Encounters in Cryptozoology.* Fresno, CA: Linden Publishing, 2002.

Coleman, Loren, and Patrick Huyghe. *Field Guide to Bigfoot, Yeti, and Other Mystery Primates Worldwide.* New York, NY: Harper Perennial, 1999.

Dennett, Preston. *Bigfoot, Yeti, and Other Ape-Men* (Mysteries, Legends, and Unexplained Phenomena). New York, NY: Chelsea House Publishers, 2010.

Hall, Mark A., and Loren Coleman. *True Giants: Is Gigantopithecus Still Alive?* San Antonio, TX: Anomalist Books, 2010.

Hillary, Edmund. *High Adventure: The True Story of the First Ascent of Everest.* New York, NY: Oxford University Press, 2003.

Meldrum, Jeff. *Sasquatch: Legend Meets Science.* New York, NY: Tom Doherty Associates, 2006.

Montgomery, R. A. *The Abominable Snowman* (Choose Your Own Adventure #1). Waitsfield, VT: Chooseco, 2005.

Teitelbaum, Michael. *Bigfoot Caught on Film: And Other Monster Sightings!* (24/7: Science Behind the Scenes Mystery Files). New York, NY: Children's Press, 2008.

Wand, Kelly, ed. *Ape-Men: Fact or Fiction?* (Opposing Viewpoints). Detroit, MI: Thomson Gale, 2006.

Willin, Melvyn. *Monsters Caught on Film: Amazing Evidence of Lake Monsters, Big Foot & Other Strange Beasts.* Cincinnati, OH: David & Charles, 2010.

INDEX

About the Authors

Turin Truet is a writer who resides in White Plains, New York.

Laura Anne Gilman, a writer and editor, lives in New York City.

Photo Credits

Cover, back cover, pp. 1, 6, 12, 19, 27, 35, 42, 48 (Yeti) © www.istockphoto.com/Michael Knight; cover, back cover, p. 1 (snow) Shutterstock; cover, back cover, p. 1 (lens) © www.istockphoto.com/jsemeniuk; p. 5 © Andrew Holt/Alamy; pp. 6, 10–11, 12, 16, 19, 22–23, 24, 27, 30, 35, 36, 42, 45, 48, 51 (trees and mountains) Shutterstock; p. 7 Sam Taylor/AFP/Getty Images; pp. 9, 15 © AP Images; p. 17 Bill O'Leary/The Washington Post via Getty Images; pp. 20, 28 Popperfoto/Getty Images; p. 25 RIA Novosti/Photo Researchers, Inc.; p. 32 Ernst Haas/Getty Images; p. 38 © Sibbick/Fortean/Topham/The Image Works; p. 40 http://en.wikipedia.org/wiki/Human_evolution; p. 44 NASA via Getty Images; p. 47 afplivetwo/Newscom; p. 49 © The Orange County Register/ZUMA Press; p. 52 Tim Mosenfelder/Getty Images; p. 54 Everett Collection, Inc.

Designer: Matthew Cauli; Photo Researcher: Amy Feinberg